The White Stallions

The Story
of the
Dancing Horses
of Lipizza

A Timestop Book
by
Laurel van der Linde

New Discovery Books
New York

Maxwell Macmillan Canada
Toronto

Maxwell Macmillan International
New York Oxford Singapore Sydney

For  valon

Design: Deborah Fillion
On the cover: The horses and riders of the Spanish Riding School
        (Photo by John Gliege)

New Discovery Books
Macmillan Publishing Company
866 Third Avenue
New York, NY 10022

Maxwell Macmillan Canada, Inc.
1200 Eglinton Avenue East
Suite 200
Don Mills, Ontario M3C 3N1

Macmillan Publishing Company is part of the Maxwell Communication Group
of Companies.

First Edition

Printed in the United States of America

10 9 8 7 6 5 4 3 2 1

Library of Congress Cataloging-in-Publication Data
Van der Linde, Laurel, 1952–
    The white stallions : the story of the dancing horses of Lipizza / by Laurel
van der Linde. — 1st ed.
        p.   cm.
    "A Timestop Book."
    Includes index.
    Summary: Traces the history of the Lipizzan breed of horses and of the
Spanish Riding School in Vienna where they received their unique training.
    ISBN 0-02-759055-0
    1. Lipizzaner horse—History—Juvenile literature. 2. Spanische Reitschule
(Vienna, Austria)—History—Juvenile literature. [1. Lipizzaner horse—History.
2. Spanish Riding School (Vienna, Austria)—History.] I. Title.
SF293.L5V36   1994   93-18919
636.1'3—dc20

Acknowledgments

Special thanks to
Sandra Heaberlin and John Gliege
of the Lipizzan Association of North America,
Laura Leafgreen and June Boardman
of the United States Lipizzan Registry,
and Mrs. Eva Podhajsky.

ontents

The horses and riders of the historic Spanish Riding School perform a school *quadrille*.

*P*rologue

He heard it. There was no mistaking the sound of the mournful, strident wail of the air-raid siren. He waited for the All Clear to sound. It didn't. Instead, the loud rumble of approaching Allied bomber planes could be heard overhead. Was it possible? Was Vienna actually under attack?

Alois Podhajsky did not have to wait long for an answer. As he ran to the stable he could hear the bombs falling on the city. He had known the Allied troops were close; neighboring cities had been attacked during the "Big Week" bombings earlier that year. As a precaution, Podhajsky had moved the younger Lipizzan **stallions** to the Lainz Zoo just outside Vienna. The older horses, however, remained at the Spanish Riding School in the heart of Vienna so that they could continue their training. After all, the Allies had spared Rome and Paris from air attack. Surely they would not bomb the cultural city of Vienna.

But they did. As the Allied planes streaked through the sky that night of September 10, 1944, the shrill scream of their bombs falling through the air struck fear into Podhajsky's heart. The lives of his rare and beautiful horses were in immediate danger. With so few Lipizzans in the world, the loss of even one would be great.

The Lipizzans had been the pride of Austria for almost 400 years. After Hitler had launched the *Anschluss* in 1938, annexing Austria and making it part of Germany, the Spanish Riding School had become part of the German army. The red-white-red Austrian flags that had hung from the two pillars in the center of the riding hall were replaced by the black swastika of the Third Reich. All the horses at Piber, the Austrian **stud** that provided the Spanish Riding School with its horses, had been ordered moved to Hostau, in what was then Czechoslovakia. It was here, at the "super stud" of Hostau, that Hitler intended to develop "super horses" for the "super people" of the New World Order.

Podhajsky reached the ground floor of the stable and began shouting orders to his staff. All 70 stallions had to be evacuated from their stalls. Recognizing the air-raid warning from practice drills, the beautiful white horses came to the doors of their stalls so they could be led away quickly.

Every member of the Spanish Riding School staff, from the groom to the head rider, scrambled to lead the horses to the safety of the air-raid shelter. Plaster fell from the ceiling of the 200-year-old stable building, some of it landing in the horses' marble feeders.

The horses had to cross the courtyard of the Stallburg in order to get to the safety of the air-raid shelter in the Winter Riding Hall. If an Allied bomb landed in the courtyard, horses and handlers would be blown to pieces. The nightmare continued for hours. Bombs exploded all around the school. Doors were ripped from their hinges, windows shattered. Podhajsky was surprised that the white stallions of Vienna stood still, in silent counterpoint to the earsplitting screams of the falling bombs. When a particularly loud explosive crashed to the ground, the horses cowered and looked confused. War didn't make sense to them. Did it make sense to anybody?

Miraculously, the Spanish Riding School survived the Allied attack on Vienna. The next morning, staff, horses, and buildings were shaken, but intact. Buildings located as close as next door had been completely decimated in the raid.

Podhajsky determined to petition the German high command to evacuate the Spanish Riding School. They must leave immediately. The end of the war was clearly at hand, with the Allied forces the obvious victors.

Much to Podhajsky's distress, his request was denied: direct orders from Berlin. If the horses were evacuated, the Germans feared the Viennese would view it as a sign of German fear and resignation in the face of the approaching Allies. These few fanatics of the Third Reich were prepared to risk the safety of Austria's national symbol in an effort to keep the Viennese morale high.

But Colonel Alois Podhajsky, director of the Spanish Riding School of Vienna, was not willing to take that risk. He had strongly objected when Hitler ordered the Lipizzan stud at Piber transported to Hostau. Even more, he opposed the breeding experiments being conducted there by Hitler's head veterinarian, Gustav Rau. The Lipizzan was a rare horse, its breeding carefully molded over the last four centuries. Breeding the horses with their close family relatives (**inbreeding**) threatened the Lipizzans' existence as much as breeding them with different breeds (**outcrossing**).

It was well-known that Hitler hated horses. Also, it didn't take a genius to understand that neither the Lipizzans nor the Spanish Riding School could survive without their own stud. Was Hitler intentionally putting the Spanish Riding School and the rare Lipizzans in jeopardy?

The bombings continued into the new year of 1945 with greater frequency. Frustrated, Podhajsky decided to take matters into his own hands. One day he noticed large moving vans in front of the museum. They were being used to move valuable art treasures outside the city of Vienna for safety. Surely it was not stretching the point to value the old pictures, saddles, and uniforms of the Spanish Riding School as highly as the museum's art treasures. And weren't the white horses thought of as living representatives of Baroque art?

This argument produced the desired response from the German high command. Podhajsky was given permission to begin evacuating part of the school. But it would have to be done in shifts, so as to not draw attention.

But where could he take the Lipizzans? Podhajsky had a friend, Countess Gabriele Arco-Valley, whose husband owned the castle of St.

Martin, 190 miles (300 kilometers) north of Vienna, in Upper Austria. As World War II swept across Europe, St. Martin had become home to more than 300 refugees. The castle had a large amount of stable space, so it was the perfect place for storing "art treasures." Orders in hand, Podhajsky arranged to move the first shift of 17 horses to safety.

Carts and wagons were loaded with the paintings and other valuable pieces of Baroque art remaining at the school. The royal Lipizzan stallions were harnessed to the wagons. Masquerading as cart animals, the Lipizzans made their way safely to the train station.

The Allies continued to bomb Vienna, and in February a second shift of 45 stallions left for St. Martin. But the few remaining horses and staff were still forbidden to leave. Podhajsky tried desperately to contact the German high command in Berlin for permission to evacuate. But telephone lines were down due to the constant air raids. Finally, Podhajsky was able to enlist the help of the German cavalry inspector, General Weingart, who managed to get the move authorized.

On the afternoon of March 6, 1945, Alois Podhajsky stood in the beautiful Baroque Riding Hall. Never before in its 200 years had the Spanish Riding School been exiled from its place of work. It had been the scene of much splendor and grace. Now its beauty was dulled by the paper put over the windows shattered in the air raids. The crystal chandeliers that usually bathed the white hall in a warm and welcoming glow had been dismantled; Podhajsky himself had ordered them removed for their safety. Would this masterpiece of Baroque architecture survive the war? Only time would tell. And at that moment, Podhajsky had to ensure the safety of the remaining horses.

This last move was fraught with peril. The trains moving out of the city were overloaded and the engineer did not want to hitch up the cars that carried the horses. Podhajsky had to use some persuasive words to get the cars with the Lipizzans attached to the train. They finally pulled out of the station around midnight.

After four torturous days and three air attacks, the Lipizzans arrived at St. Martin, joining the 62 earlier arrivals in the castle stable. All 70 stallions and the staff of the Spanish Riding School had been success-fully moved to safety. The immediate danger over, Alois Podhajsky turned his attention to an even more troubling problem: the Allies.

What could he expect from them? And which of the Allied troops would conquer Austria? The thought of the Russians was frightening, but the Americans were also worrisome. What understanding could they have of European culture and art?

Podhajsky had observed the Americans when he competed in the 1936 Olympic equestrian events. They did not regard their horses in the same manner as the Europeans, who saw the horse as living art and classical riding as an art form no less demanding than ballet.

One thing was certain: The life he had known and the 200-year-old culture of the legendary Spanish Riding School would be forever altered. With the Lipizzan **mares** and **foals** of the Piber stud isolated in Czecho-slovakia and the stallions removed to St. Martin, it was highly ques-tionable whether the Lipizzan breed would survive at all. Who could pre-dict how Europe would be divided after the war and what effect it would have on these horses?

A new world was about to be carved out of the ruins of the old. Would it be better or worse? There were no answers in April 1945. The world teetered on a political precipice, anxiously awaiting news of its fate. So did the Spanish Riding School of Vienna. So did Alois Podhajsky.

A group of Lipizzan mares and foals graze in a pasture.

Chapter 1

The Story of *Lipizza*

At first glance, the stony ground and steep hills of Lipizza might not seem suitable for raising horses. Yet in 1580 the archduke Charles II of Inner Austria chose this rocky region to found a stud. Its purpose was to provide horses for the Hapsburg royal family and the court riding school.

Lipizza is actually an oasis situated in the northernmost part of a rocky plain called the Karst. An ancient word, *karst* is derived from the Slavic words *krasen*, meaning "beautiful," and *krasota*, meaning "spectacular." The area is known today as a natural phenomenon.

The Karst is surrounded by a dry valley carved by the Reka River, which disappears underground, travels 20 miles (32 kilometers) northwest, then rises from the rocks near Aquilea as the Timav River. Local legend has it that a shrine dedicated to Diomedes, Thracian hero and god of horses, was built at the sight of the river's resurgence.

Because the Karst is located 1,300 feet (400 meters) above sea level, rain is immediately captured and taken into the depths of the earth, creating a network of underground rivers and thousands of underground caves. Twenty-nine underground caves are located in Lipizza alone, including Vilenica, one of the largest in the world. According to

13

HISTORICAL LOCATIONS OF THE WHITE STALLIONS

local legend, fairies once lived and danced behind the foggy veil that shrouds the cave's entrance.

It is possible the archduke Charles knew some of the local folklore when he selected Lipizza as the site for the royal stud. It is certain he knew the region's reputation for producing excellent horses. Since

14

ancient times the best horses had come from the Karst. Known for their speed, endurance, and versatility, these animals were prized by the Romans as both war and chariot horses.

The rough terrain generated a sturdy animal, its hooves toughened by the hard ground, its lungs developed by inhaling the clean alpine air as it conquered the rocky slopes. Though the soil was not suitable for farming, the white limestone yielded a nutritious grass that proved ideal for horses to graze upon. From these conditions emerged a horse strong enough to be the seat of army commanders, yet graceful enough to be the throne of kings.

The farming village of Lipizza took its name from the linden groves surrounding the area. Meaning "little linden tree," the name was first spelled "Lipitza." When the archduke purchased the 770-acre (308-hectare) estate, the spelling was changed to "Lipizza." Centuries later when, as a result of World War I the village became part of the Yugoslavian republic, "Lipizza" was changed to "Lipica." All three names refer to the same estate, high above the Adriatic Sea, which became the birthplace of the white horses of Vienna.

The royal stud at Lipizza grew rapidly. Only a decade after its establishment, it numbered between 60 and 70 breeding mares and had already sent 30 **colts** to the archduke Charles's stable in Graz. The Viennese court and riding school continued to demand more horses of the "Lipizza strain of the Karst breed," as they were officially called. To meet this demand, the stud had to expand, not just by producing more horses but by building more barns to house horses, hay, and stable hands. The existing estate pastures were improved and additional land was purchased to ensure enough food for the ever-increasing Lipizza herd.

By the middle of the 18th century, the number of **brood mares** housed at Lipizza amounted to 150. Throughout the 1700s the stud continued to flourish. Then, in 1793, Austria entered into war with France.

The immense French army was led by a short Corsican general on an Arabian stallion. Over the next three years Napoléon Bonaparte penetrated farther and farther into the heart of the Austrian Empire. The royal stud at Lipizza was severely threatened.

On the morning of March 22, 1797, with Napoléon's guns thundering in their ears, the stud management evacuated the Lipizzans from their birthplace and home of 200 years. Three hundred Hapsburg horses filed through Lipizza's gates that frosty morning. The march to safety would last six weeks.

Since it was early spring, the evacuation took place during **foaling season.** Sixteen mares gave birth during the course of the march. The newborns were loaded onto carts and the procession continued east to the safety of Stuhlweissenburg, then St. George.

After six months, the Lipizza refugees began the trip home. When they arrived, they found many of the stud buildings destroyed. The farm staff set about repairing and rebuilding the stud. Not one horse had been lost in the evacuation.

Over the next 13 years, two more invasions forced the Lipizzans to leave their home until Napoléon was finally vanquished. The Lipizzans, now in exile in Hungary, again headed for home. But what awaited them at Lipizza was not a pretty sight. During their absence, Napoléon had created the Province of Illyria and appointed Marshal Marmont as governor-general. For four years the "duke of Ragusa" had pillaged an already poor country. The carefully planted linden groves, nurtured over centuries, were destroyed. Also lost were the stud books, containing 115 years of breeding records. As a result of this experience, the stud now always keeps a duplicate of the records.

For the next 100 years, life at Lipizza remained peaceful. Then in August of 1916, Italy entered World War I against Germany and Austria. Anticipating what was to come, the Lipizzan horses left their home on the evening of August 18 and marched northeast toward Laxenburg, near Vienna. Mares and foals continued on to Vienna, with the foals being transferred even farther north, to the imperial stud of Kladrub, in Bohemia.

An etching depicts the training of a Lipizzan at the Spanish Riding School in Vienna during the 18th century.

World War I brought about the end of the immense Austro-Hungarian Empire. The Hapsburg family, which had ruled the empire for 500 years, went into exile.

Like their royal owners, the imperial horses suddenly had no home. Sadly, some of them were auctioned and filled the stomachs of a people ravenous from the deprivations of war.

As a result of the armistice, Lipizza now belonged to Italy, and the Italian government demanded the return of what it now considered *its* horses. In July of 1919, 107 Lipizzans were taken from their refuge in Laxenburg and removed to Italy. They became the **foundation stock** for the Italian stud of Monte Maggiore, located just outside Rome.

Thirty-seven horses joined those that had been moved to Kladrub for their safety and were incorporated into Kladrub's breeding program, which had been in existence since 1562. Kladrub now became a part of the new state of Czechoslovakia.

The 97 horses remaining at Laxenburg were given to the new—and much smaller—Austria. But the republic of Austria did not know what to do with the emperor's horses. The minister of culture respectfully declined to place the horses under his jurisdiction, even though they were considered a national art treasure. The minister of war did the same. "Well, if nobody wants them, I'll take them," said the new minister of agriculture, Moritz Herold.

A farmer by profession, Herold realized that the sturdy Lipizzans needed a hardy environment in order to thrive. It was essential that the site of the new Austrian Lipizzan stud closely duplicate that of the now Italian Lipizza as much as possible. A small village in Styria was chosen.

Piber was no stranger to breeding fine horses. It had accommodated a military stud for more than a century. The coarseness of its terrain closely resembled that of Lipizza. The mountain pastures were just as sparse, and Piber hay was similar to that grown in Lipizza. The quaint village of Piber now became the breeding ground of the white horses of the Spanish Riding School of Vienna.

Chapter 2

Development and Breed Characteristics

Since antiquity, the horses of Inner Austria's Karst had been known for their strength, agility, courage, and speed. In medieval times these qualities made them the ideal choices as warhorses and tournament mounts. Because of their great stamina and gentle disposition, they were held in high regard.

But though the Karst horses were highly esteemed, at the time of the founding of the Lipizza stud it was generally thought throughout Europe that the best horses came from Spain. This attitude undoubtedly influenced the archduke Charles in his purchase of Lipizza, for its geography closely resembled the rocky Andalusian terrain.

The horses of the Iberian peninsula were famous throughout Europe for their strength, intelligence, courage, and elegance. However, the Spanish horse did not emerge on its own. Rather, it was the result of the mixing of several breeds, the most prominent being the refined Arabian and its coarser cousin, the Barb.

The hot blood of the Arabian desert breed—the oldest purebred breed in the world—courses through the veins of all breeds of horses. The Arab was the mount of the Moor. Muslim tradition has it that when the Yeminite tribes gave five Arabian mares to the Prophet Mohammed, he was so overcome by their beauty that he raised his hands and said, "Be thou blessed, oh daughter of the wind." In the Muslim religion the wind is believed to be the breath of the soul of God, or Allah. The Arabian horse is regarded as a gift from God and protected by Him.

The princes of the Bedouin tribes valued the beautiful Arabian mares so highly, wars were fought over them. When the time came for the mares to deliver their offspring, they were brought into the Bedouin tents. The wives of the tribe lived outside until the mares had foaled. For this reason, despite its proud and fiery attitude, the Arab is extremely loyal to its owner. It is these qualities, in addition to its beauty, that the Arabian passed on to the Lipizzan.

Only with the help of these courageous Arabian horses could the Moors fulfill Mohammed's wish that Islam be spread throughout the world. In 711, the Moors easily overran Spain on the backs of their noble chargers. The coarse horses of the Iberian peninsula were no match for the swift phantoms of the desert.

Naturally, the Spaniards wanted to refine their defeated native breed with some of the qualities of the conquerors' magnificent "drinkers of the wind." During the Moorish occupation, the Arabian and Barbary horses were bred with the native Iberian horses. This resulted in the Andalusian and the Spanish Gennet. These became the horses that other European nations coveted.

Austria was no exception. Austria's emperors were, after all, direct descendants of Ferdinand and Isabella of Spain. It was only natural that the Austrian branch of the Hapsburg family would want horses as fine as the ones pulling the carriages of their Spanish cousins.

As a result, Emperor Maximilian II began importing Spanish horses to Austria in 1562. He established a court stud at Kladrub, in what is now the Czech republic. As early as 1565, Spanish horses were being used exclusively at the Viennese court and riding school, which instructed the Austrian nobles in the fine art of horsemanship. It is from these Spanish horses that the Spanish Riding School of Vienna takes its name.

However, continuing to import Spanish horses became costly, even for the Holy Roman emperor. And Kladrub alone could not meet the demands of the Hapsburg royalty. For this reason, the emperor instructed his youngest brother, the archduke Charles, to found another stud in his province of Inner Austria. While Spanish horses would certainly be used to refine the existing Karst stock, the intention was to develop a new breed, eventually eliminating the need to import horses altogether.

As a result, the Lipizzan is truly a man-made horse, created by selecting only the best of specific breeds and crossing them to achieve certain desired characteristics. Using the hardy Karst horses as the foundation stock, it was the intention of the archduke Charles to improve the native breed by crossing them with the more refined horses imported from Spain. From this cross would evolve the much-needed new breed.

After he had selected and secured the purchase of Lipizza, the archduke Charles sent Baron Hans Khevenhuller to Spain to purchase breeding horses for use at the new stud. Over the course of the next two years, Khevenhuller obtained a total of 33 Spanish horses: 24 mares and 9 Spanish stallions, 3 of which were *brincos,* "jewels" of Spanish horse breeding.

Finally a third breed, the Neapolitan, was added to the mix. Another direct descendant of the Arabian, the Neapolitan was bred in the region of Naples, Italy. Stronger, taller, and maturing later than the Spanish horse, the Neapolitan reached the height of its popularity in the 17th century. It was highly regarded as a riding horse as well as a handsome hack, pulling the carriages of Italian princes and cardinals. It is from the Neapolitan that the Lipizzan acquired the high knee action for which it is noted.

As a breed, however, the Neapolitan has died out. The increased use of gunpowder by the end of the 17th century rendered heavy armor—and therefore heavy horses—obsolete. A lighter, quicker horse was again needed: this time to evade an enemy. Horse breeding had come full circle. Yet the breeders of the Neapolitan continued to outcross with heavier Nordic breeds rather than with lighter Oriental breeds, and the Neapolitan became extinct.

These breeds, then, formed the foundation stock of what eventually became the noble horses of Lipizza. The Oriental blood of the Arab and the Barb crossed with the native Iberian horse produced the Andalusian. The Andalusian was then crossed with the mares and stallions of the Karst, as well as with the Italian Neapolitan. The result: the Lipizzan.

Over the course of the next four centuries, the foundation stock of the Lipizzan narrowed to 6 stallion lines and 14 mare families. The stal-

Sandra Heaberlin/Silver Meadows Farm

Pluto Balmora, a descendant of the oldest Lipizzan stallion line, displays the classic beauty his ancestors were known for.

lion lines, still being bred today, include the Danish Pluto, the Italians Conversano and Neapolitan, Maestoso and Favory from the imperial Kladrub stud in Bohemia, and the purebred Arabian Siglavy.

Pluto is the oldest of the six classic Lipizzan stallion lines. The stud purchased him from King Frederik II of Denmark in 1765. His offspring found immediate favor with the Austrian court and were used to pull the heavy coaches of the Hapsburg royalty. To this day, Pluto progeny mirror their legendary founder, being sturdy horses, energetic in movement, with a large "ram head."

Descended from the Neapolitan breed but with strong Arabian influence was the black Conversano. The Conversano line of Lipizzan is known to have a stately **gait,** a desirable short back, and strong, Roman head with a slightly "broken" nose, a direct throwback to its Italian ancestry.

Similarly successful was the blue-brown Neapolitan, born in Italy in 1790. The Neapolitan offspring are known to have large heads, strong ribs, and high knee action.

When the Kladrub stud was destroyed by fire in 1756, its entire herd was moved to Lipizza. As a result, two of the Kladrub stallions, Maestoso and Favory, were used successfully in the Lipizza breeding program. Lipizzans of the Maestoso line are big-bodied, with powerful movements and a slight convex "break" in the nose line. Lipizzans of the Favory line, however, tend to have a lighter build and slight concave curve to the nose.

The last addition to the six classic lines of Lipizzan stallions was Siglavy, a purebred Arabian stallion. By the beginning of the 19th century, it had become apparent that the genetic pool of breeding horses was too narrow. Since the stud did not want to breed its horses any closer than the fourth generation, an influx of unrelated blood was needed. There was also a desire to refine the shape of the Lipizzan. Since Arabian blood had such a strong influence on the Lipizzan when the breed was begun, the decision was made to find a suitable Arabian stallion.

One was found in Paris at the stud of Prince Schwarzenberg. A gray born in 1810, Siglavy was imported to Lipizza in 1816. The Seglawi strain from which he was descended is known as the most beautiful of all Arabian strains. In fact, the name itself means "beauty." Elite and elegant, when crossed with the Lipizzan mares Siglavy's offspring impressed the imperial court with their beauty, strength, and agility.

Equally important to the development of the Lipizzan breed were the mares. With the success of the Siglavy line, Emperor Franz Joseph sent an expedition to the Arabian desert in 1856 to purchase more Arabian horses. Of these, five mares left their mark on Lipizzan breeding. In addition to the native Karst mares, the remaining foundation mares came from Kladrub and private studs. Today's Lipizzan is a descendant of the remaining 14 mare lines and stallion lines, some of which have been in use for over 200 years. It is this careful and selective breeding over four centuries that makes the Lipizzan the oldest breed of horse in Europe.

In order to readily identify this proud heritage, the name of each new foal is chosen from its foundation lines. The colts are always given two names, the first from its **sire**, the second from its **dam**. For example, a colt whose sire was Favory Amorosa and whose dam was Odessa would be named Favory Odessa.

Fillies are given one name, which usually ends in an "a," such as Athena, Destina, or Gaetana. Sometimes a number is included with her name. If for example, the filly is the third in her dam's breeding line of Gaetena, she would be named Gaetena III. In order to avoid any confusion, the colts are also numbered.

Certain breed characteristics make the Lipizzan readily recognizable. To begin with, it is not a large horse. A "hand" being 4 inches, the Lipizzan averages between 14-3 (14 hands, 3 inches) and 15-2 (15 hands, 2 inches) in height. Its foreleg being shorter than its upper leg, it is known for its high-stepping strut, which allows it to excel in performing the Spanish Step, or *passage*. The Lipizzan has a well-rounded rib cage and a rather large head, though this last characteristic has been somewhat refined in the Siglavy strain. The dark eyes have an intelligent

Sandra Heaberlin/Silver Meadows Farm

A majestic head, intelligent dark eyes, and white coat give the Lipizzan its distinctive appearance.

look about them, and the tail carriage is high, another trait indicative of the Lipizzan's Arabian heritage. The hair of the mane and tail is fine and silky.

The usual color is "white," which is actually a very light gray. Lipizzans were originally of every color, including spotted piebalds. White, however, was the preferred color of the imperial court. Since ancient times, white horses were symbols of peace and justice and were dedicated to the gods. Since the Hapsburg royalty wished to emphasize these ideals, the other colors were intentionally bred out.

Laurel van der Linde/Avalon Farms

Favory Alisa II (nicknamed Amadeus), his coat still dark brown, trots beside his mother, Alisa.

Interestingly enough, the Lipizzan is not born white but dark brown, black, or mouse gray. Gradually, over a period of five to seven years, it sheds its dark coat and turns into the majestic white. The mane and tail remain dark a little longer but eventually turn white as well. However, out of every 500 or so foals born, one will stay dark brown or black. Because they are so rare, these animals are now considered very valuable. The Spanish Riding School always tries to keep one dark horse in training for good luck.

Chapter 3

The Spanish Riding School

As early as 1565, mention is made in the imperial records of a *Roßstumplplatz*, or "horse tumbling ground," a part of the palace garden where the imperial horses were trained. But the snowy Austrian winters interrupted training for both horses and riders for several months each year. Since no young nobleman's education was complete until he was an accomplished horseman, it was necessary that training continue year-round. Therefore a riding hall had to be built.

It had long been the dream of the Hapsburg monarchy to build such a hall. An imperial accounting book from 1572 lists the purchase of an order of wood for the construction of a "Spanish Riding Hall." This building was intended only as temporary housing, until the actual hall could be built.

But it wasn't until 1720 that Emperor Charles VI enlisted the services of one of Austria's leading architects, Johann Bernhard Fischer von Erlach, to design a hall for winter riding. Known as the founder of the Imperial Style, Fischer von Erlach's plans included the Riding Hall as part of the imperial Hofburg, or palace. The sight chosen was part of the palace pleasure garden, the *Paradeisgart.* Fischer von Erlach died in 1723, however, and the project was taken over by his equally talented son, Joseph Emanuel Fischer von Erlach.

A magnificent example of the Baroque era, the Riding Hall is 180 feet (55 meters) long and 59 feet (18 meters) wide, with a height of 56 feet (17 meters). Every inch of the hall is resplendent in the Hapsburg color: white. There are two galleries for observers, one lower, one upper. The 46 Corinthian columns that support the upper gallery glow in the warm light provided by three crystal chandeliers. The only source of color in the entire hall is a portrait of its builder, Charles VI, mounted—appropriately enough—on a Lipizzan. No wonder that it quickly became known as Europe's finest riding hall.

The hall was completed on September 14, 1735. Its opening was acknowledged by the arrival of "both Imperial Majesties and His Royal Highness the Duke of Lothringen, attended by all members of the high nobility." Fifty-four foals from the imperial studs were presented to the court. This was the first of many equestrian ceremonies to be held in the Winterreitschule, the Winter Riding School.

Only military officers and members of the nobility were permitted to ride at the Imperial Spanish Riding School. Trainees were accepted by special permission of the Office of the Chief Master of Horses. As the purpose of the school was—and still is—the instruction of horse and rider in the art of classical **equitation,** morning hours were reserved for training sessions. Connoisseurs of horsemanship were permitted to observe the masters at work and watched in reverence as the finest of Austria's sons learned and practiced their maneuvers.

An almost librarylike silence regularly ruled the hall. Horses and riders concentrated on their work to the rhythmic punctuations of muffled hoofbeats working against the ostinato of creaking saddles. The atmosphere was redolent with the musky smell of equines at exercise.

With the collapse of the Hapsburg Empire after World War I, the Spanish Riding School had to adjust to the times to survive. Within the

An artist's representation of riders practicing jousting with wooden heads at the Imperial Riding School.

new republic of Austria was the strong sentiment that both the Imperial Riding School and the emperor's white horses were outdated. The 300-year-old institution teetered on the brink of extinction. There was even talk of turning the beautiful Baroque Riding Hall into a movie theater or swimming pool!

But Austria's new minister of agriculture firmly believed not only in the breeding of the Lipizzans, but in the continuation of the Spanish Riding School. This was the only surviving school of classical horsemanship in the world. To lose it would be a tragedy. Moritz Herold was determined that such a heritage not be lost.

It was not an easy choice. Now that the Hapsburg monarchy was no longer paying the bills, both the stud and the school had to become self-

29

Photo: The Bettmann Archive

supporting. The government of the new republic of Austria did not even have enough money to buy brooms for the stable. What could be done?

In order to solve the immediate problem, Herold devised a "broom fund." He had postcards printed of the Lipizzans performing their most impressive maneuvers. He sold these postcards to raise money to buy the much-needed brooms. Eventually, Herold's broom fund was able to pay for other necessities as well.

As chief rider, Herold offered tours of the school to Vienna's educational groups and gave lectures on the history of the school and the work that was done there. And for the first time in its long history, the school began to give regular public performances. Visitors were eager to see the legendary Lipizzans perform their beautiful equine ballet. As a result of Herold's dedication and hard work, the school and the Lipizzans were saved and the work of centuries was allowed to continue.

Herold's successor as director of the Spanish Riding School was Count Rudolf van der Straten. Van der Straten was the emperor's last master of horse. He had fought at the front during World War I, returning to the court stables just before that war ended.

When van der Straten assumed control of the school, there were 30 horses. While Moritz Herold had certainly done an admirable job keeping the school afloat in the turbulent waters of change, additional income was needed if the school was to continue. "Art now had to go begging," said van der Straten, and he took the Spanish Riding School on tour.

The school performed first in Berlin, then Aachen, London, The Hague, and Brussels. But while these tours generated income, they also had a more far-reaching effect: By increasing the Lipizzans' exposure to the rest of the world, the white horses of Vienna became the symbol of Austria.

With the onslaught of Hitler's army, van der Straten was forced to put the school under the control of the German army. He did so and promptly resigned, recommending his position be taken over by one of his students, Alois Podhajsky.

Chapter 4

Training the *Horse*

The purpose of the Spanish Riding School is inscribed in an old stone set above the proscenium of the Baroque Riding Hall. It reads: TO BE USED FOR THE INSTRUCTION AND TRAINING OF THE YOUTH OF THE NOBILITY AND FOR THE SCHOOLING OF HORSES IN RIDING FOR ART AND WAR. It was as a means of training horses for war that the art of classical horsemanship, or **dressage**, evolved. Only in the fertile ground of the Viennese Baroque era could the seed of classical horsemanship gain enough nourishment to flower into an art form.

Dressage (pronounced like "massage") is a French word that simply means "training." But dressage is more than a way of training horses; it is an approach or philosophy as to how to work with the horse so that the horse and rider become partners. The cornerstones of classical riding are kindness, patience, and understanding. When these three principles are used, the horse, obviously a much larger and stronger animal than the human, voluntarily submits to the trainer's will.

These ideas are not new. They date back 2,400 years to Xenophon, a Greek general and statesman, who wrote two books on the subject of

31

training horses, *Hipparchikos, (The Leader of the Horsemen)* and *Peri Hipikes (Concerning Horsemanship)*. "Anything forced and misunderstood can never be beautiful," he said. "Riders who force their horses by the use of the whip only increase their fear, for they then associate the pain with the thing that frightens them."

Xenophon approached his horses with gentleness, training not only their bodies but their brains. He encouraged a horse to learn an exercise rather than forcing him to perform a maneuver without understanding it first. Xenophon conditioned his horses in the same manner in which the Greeks trained their Olympic athletes. The muscles had to be developed slowly and systematically in order to build strength and avoid injury.

In battle, a rider's hands and upper body were busy wielding a weapon against his enemy. To control his horse, then, the rider had to rely on his legs and seat. Believing that the lack of a saddle or cover on the horse's back put rider and horse in better contact with each other, Xenophon and his cavalry officers rode bareback. On the battlefield, direct communication between horse and rider was essential. It frequently meant the lives of both.

Sadly, Xenophon's methodical approach to training faded with the fall of the Greek Empire. Over the course of the next four centuries, the saddle was invented and first used by the Nubians, from the Nile Valley in Egypt. The Nubian saddle had a high **pommel** and **cantle** (front and back of the seat) so that the warrior could brace himself against the charge of an enemy.

Even so, a rider's legs tired. In India an attempt was made to give the rider some kind of leg rest. A rope was attached to the saddle, then tied around the rider's big toe. This was the forerunner of the stirrup. By the fourth century, the Huns and Mongols had reworked this idea, inventing the stirrup iron as we know it today.

With the Middle Ages came jousts and tournaments. At first the knights wore only light chain mail. But as their armor became heavier, larger horses were needed to carry the additional weight. The full plate armor of the 14th century was not only heavy but cumbersome. Harsh **bits** and long sharp **spurs** were used as aids to control the horse, so that the rider had to move his upper body as little as possible.

No armor, no matter how heavy, could withstand gunpowder, however. The use of this explosive forever altered the strategy of warfare. A light, quick cavalry horse was again needed. This meant restructuring the training of the warhorse. And in true Renaissance style, Xenophon's school of classical riding was reborn. Like horse breeding, horsemanship had come full circle.

One of the better-known riding masters of this period was an Italian, Count Cesare Fiaschi. Like Xenophon, he encouraged patience in the training of horses. He also suggested the use of a mild jointed bit in the horse's mouth. But in practice, some of Fiaschi's training methods were quite cruel. In order to get the horse to move forward, a cat or a hedgehog was tied to the horse's tail. Stirrups were made with sharp inner edges to dig into the horse's sides, and spikes were placed on the noseband of the **bridle**.

Fiaschi's best pupil was Frederico Grisone. When Grisone himself began to teach, he in turn had a star student: Giovanni Pignatelli. Pignatelli studied the training methods and riding techniques of circus performers. He observed that their work, while demanding a high degree of skill on the part of both horse and rider, was accomplished by balance and coordination. Nothing was forced.

Pignatelli incorporated elements of circus training into his teaching at the Academy of Naples, in Italy. Harsh devices were no longer used. Thanks to Pignatelli, classical riding took on a much lighter look. His influence can still be seen in the dressage arena today.

Like his teachers before him, Pignatelli, too, had a famous pupil, the Frenchman Antoine de Pluvinel. De Pluvinel refined his master's techniques even further and can be credited as the inventor of the "invisible ride."

In order for riding to be an art form, the work involved must look effortless. De Pluvinel worked to make the use of legs, seat, and reins unnoticeable to the untrained eye. Rarely did he use the whip or the spur, considering the spur in particular "a confession of failure."

At the beginning of the 18th century, the art of riding was dominated by the French. Refining the techniques of his predecessors even further, Francois Robichon de la Gueriniere earned a reputation as "the father of classical equitation." He also redesigned the saddle. Both his methods and a saddle similar to his original design are used at the Spanish Riding School today.

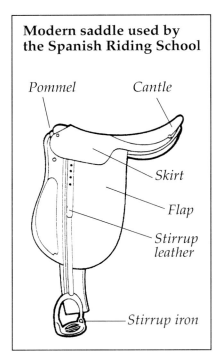

Modern saddle used by the Spanish Riding School

Pommel
Cantle
Skirt
Flap
Stirrup leather
Stirrup iron

Like its Arabian ancestor, the Lipizzan develops more slowly than other breeds. For this reason the young horses are left to play in pasture until the autumn of their third year. Then the most promising of the colts are sent to the Spanish Riding School to begin training. Fillies, on the other hand, are not put **under saddle.** Rather, they are trained to work in carriage harnesses. Only the stallions are trained in the magnificent maneuvers of the **High School**, or Haute École.

After their trip from the stud at Piber, the youngsters are led into the courtyard of the Stallburg. Here they are welcomed by the director of the school. They are then stabled in the Stallburg, taking a place where their ancestors have stood for more than 200 years. As a group, they are shown the Riding Hall and allowed to familiarize themselves with their place of work. Then, in the winter of their fourth year, the actual training begins.

For the first 8 to 12 weeks, the horse is worked on a large circle with a **lunge line**, a 30-foot (9-meter) flat line that attaches to equipment over the noseband of the horse's bridle. This work on the circle teaches the young stallion balance and coordination in all three of his gaits: the

walk, trot, and **canter**. Lunging also teaches the horse how to smoothly accomplish the transitions between these gaits.

After the horse has mastered his lessons on the lunge line, the rider is slowly, carefully, and gently introduced. Now the horse must learn to balance not only his own body but that of the rider as well. As the young horse is very unbalanced at this stage of his training, he works *only* with an experienced rider, who knows how to teach the horse how to balance its body under the working weight of the rider.

Training sessions last 45 minutes, no more. It is essential that every session end on a good note. This gives the horse a feeling of accomplishment and makes him eager to return to work the next day.

For the remainder of his first year of training, the horse continues the work of the **Lower School**. He is ridden freely forward in a natural position. This "straightforward" riding uses the full *manege*, or "working area," of the hall and further develops the horse's mind, muscles, and coordination. It also teaches communication between horse and rider. It is important that this early work be done slowly and correctly, for it lays the foundation for the horse's more advanced work. There are no short-cuts on the way to the second phase of the horse's training, the Customary or **Campaign School**.

In his second year of training, the horse begins his work in the Campaign School. Now he is asked to use his body more, performing exercises that flex his joints deeply and bend his body in smaller and smaller circles. Just like a dancer, the Campaign School horse learns to turn. Actually the pirouette is a war maneuver, used either to avoid an attacker or reverse direction for another attack. When performing the pirouette correctly, the horse's weight is carried on his hind quarters, his front or forehand lightly cantering around his almost stationary haunches.

The work of the Campaign School strengthens the muscles of the horse's hind quarters so that he can progress to the third and final phase of training. For it is the maneuvers of the High School that are the most demanding—and the most spectacular.

A horse and handler practice a *courbette* at the Spanish Riding School.

The *Haute École* includes work both on the ground as well as in the air. These moves are first taught "in hand," with the rider working the stallion from the ground. Between stationary pillars, the stallion is taught the *piaffe,* or how to trot in place. He is also taught the *passage,* or Spanish Step. The *passage* is a floating trot in which the horse seems to be suspended in the air with each stride. It takes between four and five years for the horse to master all of these moves. Only then is he ready to enter the last and most difficult phase of training.

The spectacular "**airs above the ground**" are actually cavalry maneuvers taken from the battlefield, now refined into an art form. As in the earlier work, there is a system to learning these moves.

First, the High School stallion is taught the *levade.* In this move, the horse positions his hind quarters well under his body and lifts the front part of his body, the forehand, off the ground, folding his front legs under him. His hind quarters supporting his entire body weight, the stallion holds this position for several seconds. By performing this move in battle, the horse used his body to shield his rider from enemy attack.

The *mezair* is a series of *levades* performed in sequence. After the first *levade,* the front legs are allowed to touch the ground for only a second before the horse springs forward onto his hind legs into the next *levade* and the next. Once the horse has mastered the *mezair,* he is ready to tackle one of the most difficult moves in the school above the ground, the *courbette.*

The *courbette* is a very demanding and difficult maneuver, originally designed to scatter foot soldiers on the battlefield. The horse begins the *courbette* from the *levade.* Once in position, he then jumps forward on his hind legs three to eight times in succession. His front legs never touch the ground until after the series of jumps has been completed. The number of jumps the stallion does is determined by the strength of his haunches. The record holder for the most jumps is Maestoso Borina, with ten jumps.

The *croupade* and the *ballotade* are two jumps the horse learns in preparation for the *capriole.* In both the *croupade* and the *ballotade,* the horse begins with the *piaffe*, then springs up off the ground, drawing his legs under him. The only difference between the two jumps is that in the *croupade* the horse's hind feet are tucked directly under him, while in the *ballotade* the hind hooves are angled out so that the horse's shoes can be seen from behind.

The *capriole* is an extension of the *ballotade*. Again, the move begins in a *piaffe*. The horse jumps up, but when his body achieves a horizontal position in the air, his hind legs strike out behind him, stretching to their full length before being tucked back under his body to land on all four legs. Like the *courbette*, this move harks back to the days of the medieval battlefield and was used to clear enemy foot soldiers. It is not unusual for Lipizzans to jump 5 feet (1.9 meters) in the air when performing this move.

One horse cannot master all the moves of the airs above the ground. Instead, they become specialists. For example, one horse will excel at the *courbette*, while another will specialize in the *capriole*. Each of these moves can be performed either on the long rein, with the rider guiding the horse from the ground, or with the rider astride the horse. If the airs above the ground are performed with the rider in the saddle, however, the rider does not use his stirrups, so as to not upset the horse's delicate sense of balance required for these particular moves. But, specialized training notwithstanding, the school horse must always be ready for normal riding at any time.

It takes ten years for a horse to complete his training. Only after he has mastered the moves of the High School will he be used as a breeding stallion. Every year the best stallion at the school is returned to the Piber to stand at stud for one year. This ensures that only the best horses are bred to produce the best.

None of the maneuvers of the *Haute École* can be accomplished by force. Rather, all of them are moves that the horse is capable of performing naturally or, like the *courbette*, as an extension of a natural move. When a horse is excited, it will naturally *piaffe*. On a brisk autumn afternoon or a fresh spring morning, horses will *passage*

A stallion performs a *capriole* in hand during a performance in Vienna.

39

A Tempel Farms team performs the spectacular *capriole*.

across an open field for the sheer joy of movement. Young stallions in pasture rise on their hind legs to challenge each other in play and test their bodies in the air with *caprioles* without giving the matter a second thought.

In its purest sense, then, the purpose of training is merely to teach the horse to perform on command the moves it does naturally. But in order to teach the horse, the rider must first be taught.

Chapter 5

Training the Rider

The training of the riders is as detailed and thorough as the training of the horses. In the Spanish Riding School, the training of horse and rider is handled according to an oral tradition handed down from one generation of riders to another. A slim volume of "directives" written by H. E. von Holbein was published in 1898, the year he became director of the riding school. But for the most part, the tried-and-true training methods of the Spanish Riding School are passed on directly from rider to rider.

It is not a job to be taken lightly. The trainer must learn to be satisfied and appreciative of whatever progress the horse makes, no matter how small. This requires endless patience and tremendous skill. It is not easy; but for the right person, it is very rewarding. For this reason, the Spanish Riding School chooses its rider candidates very carefully.

New riders are not accepted to the school on a regular basis. Several years may go by before there are any openings. When positions are available, they are filled quickly and always by men.

A candidate for the position of rider trainee must be at least 15 years old and have completed high school. He must also be of average height

41

and weight, so that he and the horse balance each other when they are working. As the Lipizzan is not a particularly large horse, an unusually tall candidate would not normally qualify.

Once accepted to the school, the aspiring rider is given a gray uniform and begins his training as a student, or *élève*. Days begin at five in the morning, with the *élèves* working alongside the grooms in the Stallburg, learning everything about the horse from the hoof up. The horses must be fed, groomed, and saddled before seven, for that is when they are led from the Stallburg to the Riding Hall for their daily training sessions. Lipizzans have made this parade every morning for more than 200 years. And while they file under the arched passageway connecting the Stallburg to the Hofburg, modern-day traffic stops out of respect for the tradition.

During the morning hours, the *bereiters*, or riders, train the Lipizzan stallions under the watchful eyes of the *oberbereiters*, the chief riders. These sessions are usually devoted to the older horses working under saddle. Later in the day, the *bereiter* will work the younger horses on the lunge line. Then it is time for the *élèves*.

Like the young stallions, the *élèves* begin their training on the lunge line. Riding one of the experienced horses, the trainee is taught by one of the *bereiters*. On the back of a white "professor," the *élève* works without stirrups or reins, learning to balance and coordinate his body with that of the moving horse.

Lessons on the lunge line last 45 minutes and continue for at least three months, or until the student has gained perfect control of his body in the saddle. Then, if the instructor is satisfied with his pupil's progress, he will begin work off the lunge line, learning to ride a different "professor" and using the full arena. However, his daily work on the lunge line continues throughout the remainder of the first year. But from this point on, the *élève* will ride two horses a day: one on the lunge line, the other in the *manege*.

This disciplined life continues month after month, year after year. It is very much like joining a military academy. During the course of his

John Gliege

Christine Gliege, one of the few women riders competing with Lipizzans in the U.S., prepares for a test of her riding abilities.

career as a student, the *élève* is continuously reevaluated by the director of the school. Throughout the learning process, the true character of the rider candidate is revealed. Few have the patience and dedication it takes to accomplish and maintain the high standards of the Spanish Riding School. Less than half of the rider candidates accepted to the school achieve the title of *bereiter*.

Before he can wear the bicorn hat and brown tailcoat of the *bereiter,* the assistant rider must pass a test demonstrating his riding ability. While the director of the school and the *oberbereiters* observe the candidate in the saddle, the test is really given by an experienced—and clever—school stallion.

The story is told of Neapolitano Montenuova, a stallion whose performing career spanned 20 years at the school. For capable riders, he behaved beautifully, performing all the schooling exercises intended by the rider. However, he could quickly determine the weaker riders, and when he did he resolutely brought the test to an end by executing an unexpected *capriole,* unceremoniously dumping his rider in the dirt.

Having passed the scrutiny of the stallion, the rider candidate must accomplish one more task: He must train a horse "from the ground up." Under the guidance of the *bereiters* and *oberbereiters,* the rider candidate learns how to take a young stallion, fresh from the meadows of Piber, and teach him the maneuvers used at all levels of training. There is a rule at the Spanish Riding School that a rider cannot perform in the School Quadrille unless he has trained the horse he rides. To be promoted to *bereiter* and ride in the School Quadrille is the highest recognition of achievement for both rider and stallion.

Each rider of the Spanish Riding School has between four and nine horses at different levels of training under his supervision at any given time. He works six days a week, training both horses and rider trainees. It is not an easy work schedule. Public performances are held twice a week. After the Sunday morning performance, both riders and horses take a well-deserved rest, until the training cycle begins again early Tuesday morning.

It takes 10 to 12 years for a trainee to pass through the ranks of student and assistant rider to rider. But by the time he has earned the title of *bereiter* with several horses in training, he has invested a good deal of himself in the school. It would be very difficult to leave. In some cases, generations of families have been *bereiters* at the Spanish Riding School, the tradition being handed down from father to son back three generations.

Much is to be learned from the work of this noble profession. Patience and discipline are stressed. The horse's world is simple and straightforward. The rider must understand and respect this and operate within those margins.

Modesty and self-criticism are essential ingredients, for the work is not about gratifying the rider's ego. Rather, the focus is on what horse and rider can accomplish together as a partnership. For this reason, the

An experienced rider guides his horse through a *courbette*.

The riders of Tempel Farms in Illinois salute the crowd before performing a *quadrille*.

riding crop carried by the *bereiters* of the Spanish Riding School is a simple beechwood stick, a symbol of the rider's humility before the horse. Tolerance and respect for other living creatures cannot be overemphasized.

These lessons, learned in the *manege,* can be taken outside the working arena and applied to the arena of life. Sadly, this was not the situation in 1938, when Hitler's Germany began annexing neighboring countries. With no tolerance for anything that did not mirror itself, the German Wehrmacht, or army, ran rampant, annihilating whole populations and the symbols of their culture.

The Spanish Riding School's director at the time, Alois Podhajsky, more than once questioned the activities of Hitler's head veterinarian, Dr. Gustav Rau. The Lipizzans from the stud at Piber were being cross-bred, inbred, and sold at an alarming degree. If this continued, the white horses that had become the symbol of Austria faced certain extinction. Without the Lipizzans, the Spanish Riding School faced oblivion. This living heritage is what Alois Podhajsky fought to save in the spring of 1945; not only for Austria, but for the world.

Alois Podhajsky, the legendary director of the Spanish Riding School, leads a stallion through maneuvers.

Chapter 6

The Castle at St. Martin

On the surface, the castle of Count Arco-Valley in Upper Austria seemed an ideal location to wait out the war. The imposing square castle and its outbuildings had stood for centuries as a stronghold in the middle of a large park. It was surrounded by the farming village of St. Martin, whose population normally went about its daily work in a quiet and orderly fashion. But World War II changed all that.

When the last shipment of horses from the Spanish Riding School arrived at the castle of St. Martin, they were not alone. The place was in a frenzy with the activity of other war refugees and Russian and Polish prisoners of war. By March of 1945, every able-bodied German male had been called up to fight. Those as young as 14 had been recruited to the front. Only women, children, and old men remained in St. Martin.

The Allied armies had pushed the German front back to such an extent that the refugee population of St. Martin grossly outnumbered that of the regular residents. The already limited food rations were drained. The situation had become so desperate that the Lipizzans of the Spanish Riding School were looked upon as a source of meat by the many hungry occupants of St. Martin.

To prevent the legendary horses from ending up in the village stew-pots, Alois Podhajsky called upon his experience as a soldier. Collecting what few weapons he could, Podhajsky set up lookout points and positioned his staff in both the castle and the outbuildings. All of these watch points were within sight of one another, so that the horses could be defended by coordinated crossfire. Each of these points was connected by telephone and manned 24 hours a day.

This left very little time to train the horses. Members of the Spanish Riding School staff had also been called to active service. This left each remaining rider with some ten horses in his charge. And each of these stallions was a well-muscled animal at the peak of his prime. They could not simply be shut up in the castle stable. Podhajsky tried to organize rides for the horses in the adjacent countryside, but this, too, became difficult due to constant air attacks. Routes had to be carefully chosen for immediate cover when Allied bombers were heard overhead.

The guns grew louder as the front grew closer. Viennese refugees continued to pour into St. Martin. The news they brought with them was less than encouraging. The Russians and the Americans continued to close in on the German defensive lines: the Russians from the east, the Americans from the west. Exactly where the two Allied armies would meet remained a burning question.

News came that the American advance had slowed and the Russian had accelerated. This was frightening. Podhajsky had heard what had happened to Colonel Haszlinsky and the Hungarian Riding School.

Facing the same problems as Podhajsky, Haszlinsky had evacuated the Spanish Riding School of Budapest and began moving toward Vienna. However, hearing that Podhajsky was abandoning the Viennese school, Haszlinsky decided to throw himself on the mercy of the Russian conquerors. He hoped the cultural significance of the Hungarian school would cause the Russians to put it under their protection.

His plan failed. Like the Viennese school, the riders of the Hungarian school wore German army uniforms. As a result, they were taken as prisoners of war, and 14 of the stallions were shot on the spot.

Podhajsky took action. He hid the valuables of the Spanish Riding School—saddles, gold bridles, and traditional uniforms—in the walls of the castle. So far the Germans had managed to deliver enough hay and oats for the horses on a regular two-week schedule. But as a precaution, he began to decrease the horses' rations slightly so that he would have a reserve.

Then there was the matter of the German army uniforms. Like it or not, the Spanish Riding School had been considered part of the German Wehrmacht since 1938. If they were in uniform when the conquerors arrived, the Spanish Riding School staff would certainly be taken prisoner. And as long as the Nazis held St. Martin, they had to remain in uniform.

The only choice was to play both ends against the middle. Podhajsky and his wife, Eva, quietly began to collect civilian clothes for each member of the staff. They labeled them with the riders' names and stored them in a remote room of the castle, ready to wear at a moment's notice.

In April, Cavalry Inspector-General Weingart drove his own car to the castle of St. Martin. Since he had obtained the critical papers allowing the Spanish Riding School to evacuate Vienna a month earlier, he had come to see how the refugee horses were taking to their new accommodations in exile. He had also come to say good-bye.

In his autobiography, Podhajsky recalled that Weingart watched the horses work in the makeshift *manege*. Later, he quietly walked through the stables. "You have found the best place imaginable to let the front roll over you," he said. "I am not anxious about you, for the Americans will be coming, and with your Spanish Riding School you will succeed in putting these soldiers as deeply under the spell of your white horses as you have always managed to do with me."

But Podhajsky was still concerned that the school's military position with the German army might lead to the same fate as the Hungarian school. "I am going back once more to the high command, which has now set up its headquarters in Bavaria, and will have a document drawn up for you, duly signed and sealed and to be put into immediate effect, removing the Spanish Riding School from the command of the army and declaring it once more a civil riding school. . . . This final service . . . will be the last good deed of my life."

The general continued: "We generals will be accused of allowing ourselves to become Hitler's tools, although from the beginning we were against him. . . . I am much too tired to endure again the experiences of the nineteen eighteen defeat."

As the guns grew louder, tolling the death of the great German Reich, Podhajsky received his last military orders: He was made commandant of the defensive sector of St. Martin. What did they expect him to do with a handful of young boys and old men against the fully equipped battalions of the approaching American army?

On the evening of May 2, the guns fell silent. Throughout the night a river of Nazi troops flowed through St. Martin as they retreated from the approaching American Third Army. The following afternoon, one of the riders from the Spanish Riding School rushed into the castle to report that the first American troops had arrived and seized a cart drawn by Lipizzans.

Podhajsky gave the order to have his staff change into the hidden civilian clothes. Twenty minutes later, the first American military police arrived at the castle of St. Martin and immediately began combing the grounds for German soldiers.

They also brought news of an automobile they'd found abandoned on the banks of Chiemsee Lake. The German general who owned the car had shot himself. The car fit the description of General Weingart's personal vehicle.

The Americans returned the two Lipizzans and the cart they'd been pulling. Then they rounded up all those they found in German uniforms and kept them under guard in an open field. There they awaited transportation to a prisoner-of-war camp.

But the members of the Spanish Riding School were not the only ones who thought to change into civilian clothes. The Americans now began to search for these disguised German soldiers. Podhajsky instructed his men to surrender their few weapons, then retire to their quarters and stay there.

The Americans had decided to use the castle as headquarters for the Third Army. Under the command of American officers, soldiers and local labor began making the castle ready for the occupation. The order was given to clear a large hall filled with furniture. This caused Podhajsky great alarm, for only hours before the dreaded German uniforms of the Spanish Riding School had been hidden behind this very furniture!

Eva Podhajsky decided to help the Americans clear the hall. Working a little ahead of them, she began removing the uniforms from their hiding places; she rolled them up in curtains and had them taken out in laundry baskets.

To make matters worse, the American General Collier arrived to inspect the work. This time the countess Arco-Valley came to the rescue. In order to keep General Collier from taking too great an interest in the contents of the laundry baskets, she distracted him with conversation until Eva had finished her job. It was a close call.

Meanwhile an American major had patrolled the stables and spotted Podhajsky's horse Nero, the Thoroughbred he had ridden in the 1936 Olympics. The major had seen Podhajsky ride in Berlin and win the bronze medal. He wanted to meet the Olympic medalist in person.

While Podhajsky and the major were talking, General Collier and the Twentieth Corps commander, General Walker, arrived in the stable. The major introduced Podhajsky to the generals, making them aware of Podhajsky's fame as a rider and the significance of the Spanish Riding School.

This gave General Walker an idea. He asked Podhajsky if the school could give a performance the next day. He intended to invite the under secretary of war and the commander of the entire Third Army, General George S. Patton.

Podhajsky readily agreed. This was the chance he needed. Patton was a horseman and had competed in the pentathlon in the 1912 Olympics in Stockholm. Surely a horseman of Olympic caliber would

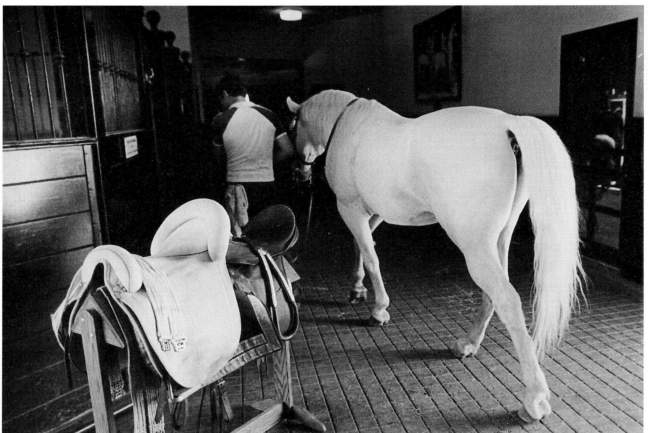

AP—Wide World Photos

A stallion is led back to his stall after a performance in Vienna.

understand the importance of the Spanish Riding School. If General Patton liked the performance, perhaps he would put the Spanish Riding School and the stud under American protection. For Podhajsky, his staff, and the Lipizzans of the Spanish Riding School of Vienna, this would be the ride of their lives.

Chapter 7

Operation Cowboy

If the Spanish Riding School was to impress the American general, there was much to do. The makeshift schooling arena needed to be dressed up with branches from the nearby woods. The courtyard and stables had to be immaculate, and the traditional uniforms, saddles, and bridles were dug out of their hiding place in the castle walls.

Then there was the problem of the horses. Given the constant upheaval of the last months of the war, their training had been maintained at a minimum. There were also fewer riders than normal for a public performance. Podhajsky had to rework the program, so he was glad to learn that General Patton would be delayed for a few days. What he did not know was that the Second Cavalry Group of the American Third Army was already in the process of rescuing the horses at Hostau.

Hostau, Czechoslovakia, sat in the eye of the raging hurricane that was World War II. While millions suffered unimaginable conditions in the Nazi death camps, life at Hostau continued in a peaceful, orderly fashion. Even the prisoners of war were well treated. Many had married into the village families and had children.

But the people of this picturesque village knew their idyllic life was coming to an end. They listened to the radio broadcasts and learned the Allies were close at hand. Who would take Czechoslovakia?

55

On April 14, 1945, the Americans reached Bayreuth, in Germany. They continued their advance and four days later were at Hof, in Bavaria, only 10 miles (16 kilometers) from the Czechoslovakian border. Then they halted. According to the agreement signed at Yalta, the Americans and Russians had determined that the Russians would take Czechoslovakia.

For those working at the stud in Hostau, this was not good news. It was well-known that the Russians had a taste for horse meat. It was at this point that the stud commandant, Lieutenant Colonel Rudofsky, received a surprise visitor. "I know a way of guiding you and your horses safely through the lines," said the mysterious Luftwaffe officer known only as Colonel "H". "However, we must act immediately." Then he disappeared.

Colonel "H" was commander of a large German intelligence unit. They had run out of fuel during their retreat, so they were bivouacked in a hunting lodge near Cheb, Czechoslovakia. The night of April 25, Colonel "H" went behind the American lines and met with the American Captain Ferdinand P. Sperl, of the Second Armored Cavalry Group. The two men negotiated the surrender of the German intelligence unit.

On the morning of April 26, Captain Sperl led an advance on the hunting lodge. This had all been arranged the night before. Both sides had agreed to aim their weapons high so the "attack" was nothing more than a mock battle. The Germans promptly surrendered, and Colonel "H" was brought before the commander of the American Second Armored Cavalry, Colonel Charles Reed.

Colonel "H" was most gracious to his American conqueror and, upon learning that Colonel Reed had missed breakfast as a result of the morning's activities, invited Reed to dine with him in the hunting lodge.

Over breakfast, Colonel "H" turned to the subject of horses. Reed, after all, was commander of the Second Cavalry Group, which had traded its horses for armored tanks only three years earlier. Clearly there would be a soft spot in the cavalry officer's heart for the fine horses at Hostau.

Colonel "H" produced pictures of the animals, the best in Europe. Reed, an expert horseman, certainly understood the problem. But the situation presented a dilemma. Though Hostau was only a few miles away, it lay across the line of demarcation specified in the Yalta agreement. If Reed authorized a move into Hostau, it would be in direct violation of that agreement.

Reed decided to put the question to his superior officer, the commander of the entire Third Army, General George S. Patton. He radioed Patton at Third Army headquarters.

Of course, Patton was more than aware of the Yalta agreement. In fact, he was outraged by it. The Yalta agreement denied the trophy of Berlin to the valiant general who had liberated Paris and led the Third Army into Germany. Why should the Russians be given the glory of taking the German capital? For this reason Patton's response to Colonel Reed's question about the horses was short and to the point: "Get them. Make it fast."

Colonel "H" now sent a message to Lieutenant Colonel Rudofsky at Hostau. Rudofsky was instructed to send staff veterinarian Rudolph Lessing through the American lines. As Lessing knew the horses in his charge better than anyone else and had a good command of the English language, he was the obvious choice to arrange for the surrender of Hostau. Around eight o'clock on the evening of April 26, Lessing arrived at the American camp. He rode one Lipizzan stallion and led another.

An agreement was reached, but Lessing warned that there was a German SS unit stationed between the American lines and Hostau. As a show of good faith, Reed agreed to send an American officer back to Hostau to help with the necessary preparations. Captain Thomas Stewart volunteered to ride behind enemy lines with Lessing. Less than 24 hours later, Lessing and Stewart returned to the American camp after some hair-raising experiences behind enemy lines, for which Stewart was later decorated.

At first light on the morning of April 28, the American frontline troops opened fire. Led by Lieutenant William Quinlivan, Task Force

Reed broke through the enemy ranks, and the town of Hostau was easily reached.

The atmosphere was festive. Townspeople and prisoners of war lined the streets, cheering. The German soldiers surrendered their weapons. The German flag came down, and the American flag went up. Yalta agreement or no Yalta agreement, the super stud of the great German Reich was now held by the Americans.

Of course, Alois Podhajsky had no way of knowing of these events, his line of communication to Hostau having been severed months earlier by the bombings. The Second Cavalry had moved into Hostau four days before the American occupation of St. Martin. But as far as Podhajsky knew, his beloved mares at Hostau were still in utmost danger. And the truth of the matter was, they were.

On the morning of May 7, the castle of St. Martin anxiously awaited the arrival of General Patton. The beautiful white stallions had been groomed to perfection, and their newly polished gold bridles sparkled in the sunshine. The riders of the Spanish Riding School wore their traditional brown tailcoats and sat astride their horses in formation just outside the working arena. Everyone shared one thought: Could the white stallions work their magic on the American general?

At eleven o'clock, General Patton's motorcade arrived. The riders and horses of the Spanish Riding School stood at attention. General Patton got out of his jeep and strode past them, raising his hand to acknowledge their salute. Accompanied by his entourage of four generals, four colonels, and Undersecretary of War Patterson, Patton took his seat in the hastily built grandstand. Now the performance could begin.

The white stallions danced to the recorded music Podhajsky had had the foresight to bring from Vienna. First, two horses and riders performed a *pas de deux*, or dance for two. Podhajsky studied Patton's face for a response. The horses and riders were doing well, but the general looked bored.

Now the horses performed the "airs above the ground." As they leapt into *caprioles*, *courbettes*, and *levades*, the general became interested.

U.S. Army photo courtesy of the Patton Museum, Fort Knox, KY

Colonel Alois Podhajksy addresses General George Patton at the performance that convinced him to save the horses during World War II.

Next came the work on the long reins, and finally Podhajsky performed a solo on Neapolitano Africa. He finished by riding in *passage* to face General Patton directly. Podhajsky halted; General Patton rose. The fate of the Spanish Riding School hung on this moment. Podhajsky took off his bicorn hat and spoke.

> "Honorable Mr. Secretary and General. I thank you for the great honor you have done the Spanish Riding School and myself by your presence. The Spanish Riding School, this ancient Austrian cultural institution, is today the oldest riding school in the world and has managed to survive wars and revolutions throughout the centuries and by good fortune has lived also through the recent years of

upheaval. The great American nation, which has been sin-
gled out to save European culture from destruction, will
certainly interest itself also in this ancient academy, which
with its riders and horses presents, as it were, a piece of
living Baroque, so I am sure I shall not plead in vain in
asking you, General, for your special protection and help;
for protection for the Spanish Riding School, which will
pass the difficult period of transition under American military command, and for help to locate and bring back the
Lipizzan stud, which is at present in great danger on
Czechoslovakian territory."

Of course, at this point, Patton knew more about the mares in
Hostau than did Colonel Podhajsky, the American occupation of the
stud having taken place nine days earlier. After a short whispered conversation with Undersecretary Patterson, General Patton gruffly
announced that he was putting the Spanish Riding School under American protection.

Podhajsky was overjoyed. As a gesture of thanks, Podhajsky invited
the general to tour the stables. Patton readily agreed and took great
interest in the horses as he reviewed them in their stalls. Podhajsky
hoped to have another opportunity to question the general about the
horses in Czechoslovakia.

When he did bring up the subject again, Patton asked one of his
aides to bring him a map. Podhajsky pointed to Hostau. Since the two
men spoke through a translator, it is likely that Patton did this to con-
firm that the horses Podhajsky was concerned about were the same
ones the Second Cavalry had already secured. Before General Patton
left St. Martin, he left strict orders that the safety of the Lipizzans was
to be a priority.

It was a good thing he did, for despite the American occupation of
Hostau, the Lipizzans were not out of danger. Second-in-command at
Hostau was a Czech-born lieutenant colonel. This man still clung to

U.S. Army photo courtesy of the Patton Museum, Fort Knox, KY

General Patton salutes the horses and riders of the Spanish Riding School after their performance.

Nazism. When the preparations for the surrender of Hostau were being made on April 27, the Czech objected but could get no one in the stud to support him. What no one knew was that he and the Russian communists were secretly plotting against the American conquerors.

Shortly after Germany officially surrendered on May 7, Colonel Reed became aware of the communist conspiracy at Hostau. Greatly concerned, he once again contacted General Patton, recommending that the horses be moved immediately. There was no time to separate the Lipizzans from the other horses at the stud, so the order was given to have an old-fashioned roundup and move them—all 1,000 of them.

Operation Cowboy got underway at dawn on the morning of May 12, 1945. The few trucks available were used to transport the pregnant mares and foals. The rest were divided into small herds and the move to Schwarzenberg was begun.

On May 14, Alois Podhajsky took the first airplane ride of his life. General Patton had requested that Podhajsky get to Schwarzenberg as quickly as possible to review the Lipizzans. Podhajsky was flown to Zinkovy, where he met Colonel Reed. Over dinner, Reed informed Podhajsky that the captain of the United States riding team had seen Podhajsky ride in the 1936 Olympics and was so impressed that he named a horse in the cavalry school after him. In addition, Reed's brother had also named his horse after the Olympic medalist and had achieved a good deal of success with that horse. Horseman to horseman, the two men were now on common ground.

The next morning, Reed drove Podhajsky to Schwarzenberg to inspect the horses. Podhajsky selected the horses that were formerly at the stud in Piber. They numbered 215 in all, and arrangements were then made to move these animals to a location 2.5 miles (4 kilometers) from St. Martin.

The horses were moved in two groups: one on May 18 and one following on the 25th. General Patton again intervened, issuing an order that the Lipizzans were to be given priority on all roads during the move. It was not easy.

The roads used to make the 200-mile (322-kilometer) trip had also suffered the effects of war. They were very rough to travel, and in some places bridges had been blown up. Podhajsky had not chosen any of the Lipizzans that had come to Hostau from other countries. The Lipizzans from Italy were returned to their country, as were the Yugoslavian horses. To Lipica, birthplace of the breed, only 11 horses were returned.

Epilogue

At the end of the war, the Spanish Riding School left the castle of St. Martin and took up temporary residence in Wells, Austria, the boyhood home of Alois Podhajsky. The peace negotiations dragged on and ten years passed before the Spanish Riding School could return to its home in the Hofburg.

Little by little, the horses Podhajsky had selected at Schwarzenberg were returned to Piber. The careful breeding of the Lipizzan for the Spanish Riding School was begun again.

But some of the Lipizzans had many more miles left to travel. Nine Lipizzans were selected as war booty and were shipped to the United States, along with 134 other horses collected from the European campaign. After a very rough ocean crossing, the horses disembarked at Newport News, Virginia, in October of 1945. They were taken to Front Royal, Virginia, where they spent the winter. The following April they were shipped by train to the Kellogg Ranch in Pomona, California. William Keith Kellogg had been raising Arabian horses there since 1925. In 1943, wishing to make a contribution to the war effort, the cereal king had given the property to the American military, making it a remount depot.

But the American military no longer needed cavalry units. After centuries of indispensable service on the battlefield, the horse was no longer needed. The remount depot in Pomona was closed in 1948 and the horses were sold at auction. The Lipizzans that entered the United States as prizes of war remained in the country after they were sold.

But there were other independent Lipizzan stud farms beginning to emerge. In 1958, Tempel Smith of Tempel Steel purchased 20 Lipizzans from Piber and imported them to his 7,000-acre farm in Wadsworth, Illinois. Planning to develop a purebred Lipizzan breeding program, Smith purchased six mares from Hungary in 1964, along with three stallions and three mares from Lipizza. Five Hungarian stallions trained at the Spanish Riding School were added later.

The Tempel Farm herd grew. Twenty years after its founding, the herd numbered more than 500 horses. While it no longer maintains such a large collection of horses, Tempel Farm Lipizzans have kept some important company. Among other things, they were part of the inaugural parade when former president Ronald Reagan was sworn into office in 1981.

Meanwhile, Ralph and Evelyn Dreitzler imported their first Lipizzan stallion to their farm in Snohomish, Washington, in 1960. In the fall of that same year, Raflyn Farms purchased one more stallion and four mares with which to begin their breeding program.

In 1962 three more Austrian mares were added to the Raflyn herd. Now all six stallion lines were represented, with the pedigree of each horse traceable to original Lipizzan foundation stock.

But all this careful planning came to a tragic end on December 3, 1975. The Snohomish and Pilchuck rivers overflowed their banks, causing massive flooding. A dam burst, and Raflyn Farms was destroyed. All the horses drowned, save two. One of those died a year later from complications resulting from the flood.

Evelyn Dreitzler hoped to rebuild Raflyn Farms at a different location but died before this could be accomplished. In 1989 her son, Ralph, fulfilled his mother's wishes and re-established Raflyn Farms in Snohomish, Washington. An operation of smaller scale, it is located on the top of Clearview Hill.

Over the last 200 years, the saga of the Lipizzans has been one of drama and tragedy. If only the story of these fairy-tale horses could have a fairy-tale ending. But their difficulties are far from over. For in

1991, their birthplace was again traumatized by war.

Since the end of World War II, Croatia had been one of the six Yugoslavian republics. Controlled by the communists, the Serbian and Croatian people were forcibly integrated. This created a significant undercurrent of unrest between the two ethnic groups.

But then the Union of Soviet Socialist Republics dissolved in the summer of 1991. With the crumble of communist rule, Croatia announced its independence from the communist satellite of Yugoslavia. The political pressure cooker exploded when the Serbs, backed by the Yugoslavian federal army, opposed Croatia's move.

Immediately, the Serbs began military action against Croatia, conquering a section of Croatian territory along the Serbo-Croatian border. The Croats retaliated, driving the Serbs into retreat. However, in the course of falling back, they destroyed everything in their path that was of significance to the Croats. This included the pride of the Croatian people, the stud farms of the Lipizzan horses.

There were three Lipizzan studs in Croatia at the beginning of the civil war: Djakovo, Lipic, and Lovas. The largest of these was Djakovo. Founded in 1506, Djakovo was Europe's oldest stud farm, originally breeding Arab-Oriental horses. It housed the Hapsburg horses for a year during their second Napoleonic exile in 1806. When the imperial stud returned to Lipizza, a few mares and stallions were left behind, thereby forming the foundation stock for Djakovo. Since 1854, Djakovo had bred only Lipizzans.

Of the three Croatian studs, Djakovo suffered the worst. It was completely destroyed by the Serbs. Ninety brood mares were killed and found buried in a mass grave. There were no survivors.

Lipic, the second-largest Croatian stud, fared little better. Like Djakovo, Lipic had been used as a stud for many years, though not always for the Lipizzan. Over the last 20 years, however, Lipic had become a stud dedicated to breeding purebred Lipizzans. It maintained about 200 horses.

Lipic was almost completely destroyed by Serbian bombs and mines.

The stud building that housed the stallions was full of bullet and mortar holes. Most of the roof was burned, and 18 Lipizzan stallions died in their stalls in the fire.

The farm workers at the Lipic stud were mostly Serbian. They had been warned by the Serbian army as to when they were going to attack the stud. As a result, the Serbian workers made themselves scarce at the scheduled time, leaving the horses defenseless.

The few workers remaining at the stud did their best to evacuate the animals. But they were able to do little more than open gates, allowing the frightened horses to escape into open paddocks and fields. Some were machine-gunned as they ran, some were captured by the Serbian army, and some managed to escape and were relocated to other parts of the country. The total number of horses lost from the Lipic stud was estimated to be around 110. The horses captured by the Serbs were reported to have been the best bloodstock. The Croatian government hopes to negotiate with the Serbian government for their return.

The smallest stud, Lovas, did not suffer the bombing and artillery fire like that unleashed on Djakovo and Lipic. However, the Serbians did steal 70 or 80 of the best horses. Here, too, the Croatian government hopes to obtain their release. But the Serbians, like the Russians who captured the Hungarian Riding School during World War II, are known to have a taste for horse meat.

The Croatian veterinarians found themselves working long hours in an effort to save the horses that did manage to escape. Many of the horses suffered from burns and shrapnel wounds. The Serbs used bullets that had been outlawed by the Geneva Convention. The bullet has a soft tip that leaves a small entry hole, but then explodes, leaving a very large exit hole and many metal fragments inside the horse.

Yet the people of the newly independent republic of Croatia remained optimistic. Having a deep pride in and a deep love for their country's horses, they were not at all distressed at finding refugee horses on their doorsteps. Though they may not have known the owner of the horse or even if that owner was still alive, their overriding concern was for the

John Gliege

Dr. Jaromir Oulehla, the current director of the Spanish Riding School.

animal. In some areas where there were no phone lines, they would summon a vet by tying a blue rag or ribbon to a tree or mailbox. This signaled a vet that he was needed at that property, so he would stop there when he made his rounds.

The front of the Yugoslavian civil war moved east from the Croatian territory to Bosnia, 60 miles (97 kilometers) from the decimated stud of

Djakovo. The dwindling ranks of the Lipizzans were once again threatened, as the 89-year-old stud of Vucijk lay within the area of military conflict.

At the start of this war, the number of purebred Lipizzans in the world was just under 3,000. We will probably never know the exact number of these rare horses lost in the civil war. The loss of even one is tragic. As was the case during World War II, the survival of the breed hangs in the balance.

Why this particular breed of accomplished, graceful, and gentle animals has consistently found itself at the center of political crisis for the last 200 years remains a mystery. The Lipizzan represents a history and a heritage, not only for Austria but for the world. The dancing white stallions of Vienna are truly living art, and the work they do at the Spanish Riding School is an art form.

Art is a reflection of mankind's nobility, sensitivity, and creativity. It transcends political boundaries, elevating mankind to a new level of understanding. The Lipizzan is one of mankind's finest creations. It and its work must be preserved, not only as a reminder of what has been but as an inspiration for what can be accomplished.

Sandy Heaberlin/Silver Meadows Farm

One of the stallions of Silver Meadows Farm, where the Lipizzan legacy continues.

Glossary

AIRS ABOVE THE GROUND The final phase of a horse's training at the Spanish Riding School. All movements are performed with at least two legs, if not all four, off the ground.

BIT A piece of either metal or rubber that is attached to the bridle and the reins and is placed in a horse's mouth to assist in balancing the horse's head and guiding its head while riding.

BRIDLE A piece of equipment that is placed over a horse's head and to which the reins and bit are attached.

BROOD MARE A mare used for breeding purposes.

CAMPAIGN SCHOOL Also called the Customary School, this is the second phase of a horse's training. Here the horse is taught to bend its body and flex its joints, shifting its balance deeper into its hindquarters in preparation for performing more difficult maneuvers.

CANTER A bounding pace in which three distinct hoofbeats are heard. If a horse is cantering to the right, it would begin on its left hind leg, followed by the right hind and left front legs striking the ground simultaneously. The right front leg would then strike the ground alone. The process is reversed for a canter to the left.

CANTLE The back part of a saddle's seat.

COLT A young male horse between the ages of birth and five years.

DAM The mother of a foal.

DRESSAGE A French word meaning "training." It is taken from the French verb *dresser,* which means "to train." *Dressage* is both a systematic method of training horses and a philosophy of kindness and humane treatment that results in a union between horse and rider. In *dressage* nothing is forced. The horse is trained so that it understands the movements it is asked to perform. This allows the horse to perform in a relaxed, balanced, and natural manner.

EQUITATION A rider's skill at performing required maneuvers with a horse.

FILLY A young female horse between the ages of birth and four years.

FOAL A baby horse of either gender.

FOALING SEASON The time of year when new foals are born; usually early spring to midsummer.

FOUNDATION STOCK The horses, male and female, on whose blood lines a breeding program is established.

GAITS The ordinary and natural paces of a horse in movement. There are three gaits—the walk, the trot, and the canter.

HIGH SCHOOL Also called *Haute École.* The third phase of a horse's training. Here it is asked to further bend its body and flex the joints of the hindquarters. The movements learned in the two previous schools are refined, and more difficult moves are introduced.

INBREEDING Breeding closely related horses with one another, such as a sire to a daughter, a dam to a son, or a brother to a sister. This type of breeding eventually produces inferior stock.

LOWER SCHOOL In the Spanish Riding School, the lower school involves the early training of horses, in which the horse is trained to become used to a saddle and rider. In this stage of training, the horse is ridden in a natural, relaxed way and is not asked to bend much.

LUNGE LINE A flat line, approximately 30 feet (9 meters) in length, that attaches to a horse's bridle and is used when training a horse in a $65\frac{1}{2}$ foot (20 meter) circle.

MANEGE The working area where a horse is trained.

MARE A female horse over the age of four.

OUTCROSSING Breeding two different breeds (such as a Lipizzan with an Arab) in order to strengthen an existing line of horses or to achieve certain desired characteristics in the offspring.

POMMEL The front part of a saddle's seat.

SIRE The father of a foal.

SPUR In *dressage*, a metal piece with a blunt end that is strapped to the heel of a rider's boot. The spur is used only in later training to ask the horse for greater bending or deeper flexing of its joints and muscles. It is *not* used to make a horse go more quickly.

STALLION A male horse over the age of five.

STUD A stallion use   for breeding purposes. Also, a farm where horses are bred.

TROT A pace in which the horse moves its legs in diagonal pairs so that only two hoofbeats are heard. In a trot, the right front and left hind legs move together, as do the left front and right hind legs.

UNDER SADDLE A term used to describe the horse's progress in training from early work on the lunge line to being ridden.

WALK A pace in which the horse moves its legs so that four distinct hoofbeats may be heard. Two or three feet are on the ground at any given time.

Index